EINSTEIN'S WATCH

EINSTEIN'S WATCH

BEING AN UNOFFICIAL RECORD OF A YEAR'S MOST OWNABLE THINGS

JOLYON FENWICK & MARCUS HUSSELBY

PROFILE BOOKS

First published in Great Britain in 2009 by

PROFILE BOOKS LTD
3a Exmouth House
Pine Street
London EC1R 0JH
www.profilebooks.com

A CIP catalogue record for this book is available from the British Library.

ISBN 978 1 84668 344 2

Text design by Jolyon Fenwick and Marcus Husselby
Typeset in Baskerville 10
Printed and bound in Great Britain by Butler Tanner & Dennis Ltd, Frome, Somerset

Disclaimer

For Philip Morris and Tom Gallaher

Foreword

The most ownable things. A category you could naturally assume was already calibrated by price. But price, dictated by those with the wherewithal and willingness to pay it, is an unreliable instrument in determining value. So on whom should one rely for this onerous task? It must clearly be left to your own careful and personal assessment. But in the meantime, if 'stuff' rather than experience could 'fill the unforgiving minute' (in the way that we think Kipling intended), then we humbly submit the following for your consideration.

All the items contained within this book were sold, offered for sale or available during the period July 2008 to June 2009.

Jolyon Fenwick
Marcus Husselby
July 2009

'This isn't life. This is just stuff.'

Lester Burnham, *American Beauty*, 1999

Einstein's watch

A tonneau-shaped 1930 wristwatch in 14K yellow gold by Longines of
Switzerland (no. 4876616, case no. 66968). Presented to Albert Einstein
in Los Angeles on 16 February 1931. Initially estimated at $25,000–$35,000,
it made the highest price ever for a Longines watch at auction – being sold
on 16 October 2008 by Antiquorum in New York for $596,000.

Playboy, **Braille edition**

1970–1985 collection of the Braille edition of *Playboy*. Since 1931, the National Library Service (NLS), a division of the US Library of Congress, has provided a free national library programme of Braille and recorded materials for blind and physically handicapped persons. Magazines included in the NLS's programmes are selected on the basis of demonstrated reader interest. Since 1970, this has included the publishing and distribution of a Braille edition of *Playboy*. The state-sponsored publication of the magazine ceased briefly in 1985 after a Congressional ban on account of its 'lack of literary merit'. This wanton act of prohibition was quickly reversed, however, and *Playboy* in Braille continues to be produced to this day. Offered for sale on eBay in May 2009. Starting bid $300.

Eiffel Tower staircase

20-step section of the Eiffel Tower staircase. The helical structure is 3.5m high, 1.7m diameter, and weighs over 700kg. Part of a section removed to allow the installation of lifts, it is likely to be the last piece that will ever be made available to the public. Sold at auction by Drouot in Paris on 13 October 2008 for €80,500.

The Queen's head

1966 plaster cast by sculptor Arnold Machin, used to create the effigy of Her Majesty The Queen's head on British stamps. Machin worked on a number of photographs of the Queen to produce a clay model bust, spending several months painstakingly tweaking the piece until it met with royal approval. His original design showed only the Queen's head, but Her Majesty insisted it also include her shoulders and dress. Another late change was to remove the words 'Postage & Revenue', so that only the Queen and the stamp value appear. Of only four original casts remaining in existence, three are held by the Royal Mail. A fourth was later found in a cupboard at Garmelow Manor, the sculptor's family home in Staffordshire. Stamp historian Douglas Myall said, 'The Queen very much liked the design, calling it a work of rare quality. When in 1984 it was suggested the image be updated, Her Majesty didn't see the need.' Machin's cast has been used to create over 320 billion stamps during the last 43 years, making it the most replicated work of art in history. Sold at auction by Cuttlestones Fine Art Auctioneers of Penkridge, Staffordshire, in September 2008 for £15,700.

King Kong's head

Handcrafted plaster, pre-production model head of King Kong, sculpted by pioneer of motion picture special effects, Willis O'Brien (1886–1962). In his creation of Kong, O'Brien drew on 'real' nature. He consulted with the zoologist at the American Museum of Natural History (obtaining the exact measurements for a bull gorilla) and studied slow-motion film research that chronicled the movement of animals in order to achieve life-like motion in stop-action animation. As well as this attention to animal realism, however, O'Brien was careful to 'humanise' his great monkey. Kong walks like a man and is capable of a far greater repertoire of facial expressions than would be found in a real gorilla. One of the earliest renditions of Kong by O'Brien, the cast features the attached teeth and intricate facial detail of what was to become the most famous movie beast in history. Sold at auction by Christie's in Rockefeller Plaza, New York, in July 2008 for $5,000.

Apollo 11 lunar surface map

Used by Apollo 11 astronauts Neil Armstrong and Buzz Aldrin to accurately determine the position of *Eagle* (the lunar module named after the US national bird) after the lunar landing in 1969. Signed and inscribed on the reverse by Aldrin. The extra-terrestrial A–Z was offered for sale at auction by Bonhams in New York on 16 June 2009. Estimate: $70,000–$90,000.

A ticket to space

Entitling a passenger to travel 110km into space, a trip estimated
to take place in 2010. Officially offered for the first time in 2009 by Virgin
Galactic, this suborbital spaceflight starts with three days of medical checks
and training covering safety procedures and all aspects of space travel,
including G-force acclimatisation. This will initially take place at Virgin
Galactic's base in the Mojave Desert. On the day of the flight, astronauts
will board SpaceShipTwo (SS2), which will then be hitched to the
'mothership', WhiteKnightTwo (WK2), which will fly SS2 to 50,000
feet, where it will be air launched. After accelerating to a speed of Mach
3.3 in just 30 seconds in a vertical ascent, SS2 will slow down to travel
110km into space, at which point passengers may leave their seats
to float in zero gravity and enjoy views of space and the Earth below
from the large windows. A ticket to space can be acquired through
elegantresorts.co.uk for $200,000.

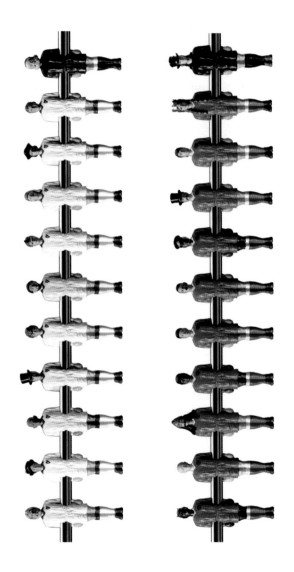

'Good versus Evil' football table

'Good versus Evil' Opus football table conceived by 20ltd.com, constructed by The Eleven Forty Company. Lacquer-finished maple wood cabinet, toughened frosted UV etched glass pitch, telescopic aluminium rods with brass castings, ergonomically designed handles and aluminium, hand-painted players with die-cast heads. The table convenes a match between 'Good' and 'Evil'. The ball is fashioned as the world, and it's souls not goals that are at stake. The teams line up as follows (left to right):

GOOD XI: God, Poppins, M. K. Gandhi, Jekyll, Robin (Christopher), Assisi, Gordon (Flash), Teresa, More (Sir Thomas), Moore (Sir Bobby), Claus (Santa).

EVIL XI: Lucifer, Caligula, Impaler (Vlad the), Hyde, Pot (Pol), Hitler, Amin, Ripper (Jack the), Klebb (Rosa), Macbeth (Lady), Catcher (The Child).

Offered for sale in June 2009 by 20ltd.com for £17,000.

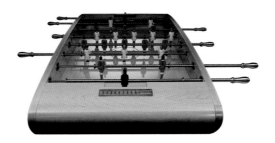

Lucian Freud's *Bacon*

Oil on canvas, 1956–1957. Unfinished painting by Lucian Freud
(born 1922) of his friend Francis Bacon (1909–1992). Sold at auction
by Christie's on 17 October 2008 for £5.4 million.

Key to *Titanic* binoculars storeroom

The key, with tag reading 'Crows Nest Key Telephone', designed to open the binoculars storeroom on the RMS *Titanic*. Fatefully, however, the key was not on the ship when she set sail from Southampton on 10 April 1912, but instead in the pocket of an officer transferred off the vessel days before its maiden voyage. He had forgotten to hand it to his replacement as he left. As a result, spying for obstacles was left to the naked eye. Mr Frederick Fleet, one of the lookouts on the ship, told the inquiry into the sinking that with binoculars the *Titanic* might have been able to dodge the iceberg. On the difference the binoculars might have made, he said: 'Well, enough to get out of the way.' The key was sold at auction by Henry Aldridge & Sons in Devizes on 21 September 2008 for £90,000.

1957 Ferrari 250 Testa Rossa

Scaglietti-designed 'pontoon-fender' 250 Testa Rossa built by Ferrari in 1957. One of only 22 to be manufactured, the car (with chassis number 0714TR) is considered one of the most competitive racing Ferraris ever built, having won ten races in North and South America between 1958 and 1961. It boasts a 300bhp, 2,953cc single overhead cam V-12 engine, six Weber 38 DCN carburettors and a four-speed manual gearbox. Sold by RM Auctions in association with Sotheby's at the 'Ferrari Leggenda e Passione' in Maranello, Italy, in May 2009 to a telephone bidder for €9,020,000 (approximately £7,655,000), making it the most expensive car in history. The previous auction record was held by a 1961 Ferrari 250 GT SWB Spyder California, previously owned by James Coburn, bought in 2008 by UK radio host Chris Evans for €7 million.

Picture copyright Darin Schnabel/RM Auctions

Del Boy's van

1972 yellow Reliant Regal bearing the legend 'Trotter's Independent
Trading Co. New York Paris Peckham'. Used in the long-running
BBC series *Only Fools and Horses*. Sold at auction at the Royal Horticultural
Halls, London, in March 2009 for £6,325.

Pat Garrett's gun

Engraved Colt Thunderer model 1877 double-action revolver. Presented to lawman Patrick F. Garrett in 1902, some two decades after he shot down Billy the Kid, by 'friends of the Custom House' at El Paso, Texas, in appreciation of his service there as United States Collector of Customs, by appointment of President Theodore Roosevelt. Sold by Rock Island Auctions of Moline, Illinois, on 7 September 2008 for $138,000.

'Bat-zooka'

A 'Sonic-Blaster Zero M' toy gun made by Mattel in 1964 that was customised into the 'Bat-zooka'. Weapon used by Burt Ward as 'Robin' or 'The Boy Wonder' ('Dick Grayson') in ABC Television's 1966–1968 *Batman* series. Given to Burt Ward as a gift from the props department and signed by the actor in silver ink, the 35-inch Bat-zooka was offered for sale at auction by Bonhams on 14 June 2009. Estimate: $2,000–$2,500.

Kate Moss's bed

Pine double bedstead, handmade by Yells of Fairford. The bed occupied the master bedroom of a Cotswold cottage in Southrop, Gloucestershire, which Miss Moss rented between 2001 and 2004. Sold at auction in November 2008 by Moore Allen & Innocent in Cirencester for £260.

Holy water sprinkler by Parker

Parker VP 1963 aspergillum (holy water sprinkler) in box: black converter-filler, frosty Lustraloy cap, gold filled trim, sprinkler in shape of chalice. Clearly once belonging to the Rev. Stanley Przybylowicz. Offered for sale by vintagepens.com for $365.

Obama posters by Shepard Fairey

Barack Obama campaign posters 'Progress' and 'Hope', and the official Presidential Inauguration poster by Shepard Fairey. In support of Obama's bid for the White House, illustrator and artist Shepard Fairey created two 24" × 36" silkscreen posters bearing the stylised image and slogans of the Illinois senator (a process that took him one day) and sold them through his website for $50. The image then went viral and became one of the iconic symbols of the campaign. Following Obama's victory, the Presidential Inaugural Committee commissioned Fairey's design for the official inaugural poster, and these posters were sold for $100 each. An edition of 1,000 prints, signed and numbered by the artist, went for $500 each. A mixed media collage of the image was snapped up by the Smithsonian, making it the first official image of the president to be inducted into the US National Portrait Gallery.

Enola Gay pilot's uniform

The uniform of Colonel Paul Tibbets, pilot of the B-29 aircraft
Enola Gay, as worn by him during the atomic bomb attack on Hiroshima
on 6 August 1945. Tibbets's aircraft carried the bomb, and was named
after his mother, Enola Gay Tibbets. The uniform is adorned with Tibbets's
Distinguished Service Cross. Sold by Alexander Autographs of Stamford,
Connecticut, on 7 November 2008 for $250,000.

Alexander Sims

Aged 21, Alexander is touted as the next 'Lewis Hamilton' or 'Jenson Button'. He is currently racing in the 2009 Formula 3 Euroseries, the acknowledged feeder series to graduate to GP2 and Formula 1. This is the same ladder to the top as used by Lewis Hamilton himself. Like many current Formula 1 drivers, Alexander is a multiple Karting champion and has received the highest recognition possible in being awarded the McLaren Autosport Award in 2008. Previous winners of the award include David Coulthard, Oliver Gavin, Ralph Firmin, Jenson Button and Anthony Davidson. Alexander is also a member of the BRDC Superstars and the MSA Elite driver development programmes. A 20 per cent share of all Alexander's future earnings from Formula 1 is currently on offer for the sum of £1.2m.

Continental shelf

In 1867, Russia sold Alaska (then presumably deemed an inconvenient lump of ice) to the USA for five cents per hectare. When gold was later discovered beneath the region's chilly expanses, the Russians unsurprisingly went a deep shade of their latter-day political colour. It is perhaps with this blunder in mind that the coastal states of the world are now engaged in a colossal land – or sea-bed – grab for so-far unclaimed areas of the ocean floor. The climax of this rather unseemly rush for sub-aqua territory came with the 13 May 2009 deadline for lodging claims to extensions of the continental shelf. The 1982 United Nations Convention on the Law of the Sea dictated that all countries that had ratified the treaty before 13 May 1999 had ten years in which to claim any extension of their continental shelf beyond the normal 370km, so long as that extension was no more than 100 miles from the point at which the sea reached a depth of 2.5km, and no more than 350 miles from land. Countries lucky enough to meet the criteria to the satisfaction of the Commission on the Limits of the Continental Shelf can then exploit the minerals on or under the seabed in this margin, so long as any revenue is shared with poorer and landlocked states. No new rights are given over fish or other creatures in the water column, but living creatures on or below the seafloor that are immobile 'at the harvestable stage' (such as sea cucumbers, which are already being garnered for the potential treatment of cancer) are treated like minerals. So far, 49 countries have made claims, with Britain asserting claims over areas in the Celtic Sea and the Bay of Biscay, and off Ascension Island, the Falklands, South Georgia and the South Sandwich Islands. Yet, as one might anticipate, the allotment of these damp boundaries is being as keenly contested as those on dry land. Argentina is competing with Britain over the Falklands; China with South Korea over a part of the East China sea; Tanzania with the Seychelles over an area near Aldabra; Canada with France over St Pierre & Miquelon; while Canada, the USA, Russia, Norway and Denmark are jostling for control of the Arctic, which may prove the most valuable prize of all. While no actual money changes hands for securing these rights, the funds expended on research, petitions and procedure are expected to run to many hundreds of millions of dollars.

Picture: Titanium Russian flag on the seabed, 4km below the North Pole

Mindarus Harringtoni

In August 2008, Dr Richard Harrington, a scientist and vice-president
of the Royal Entomological Society of London, bought a fossilised aphid
on eBay for £20. The insect, 3–4mm long and encased in a 40–50 million-year-
old piece of amber, was sent to Danish aphid expert Professor Ole Heie, and
was then confirmed as a new species, now extinct. Dr Harrington was inclined
to call the bug Mindarus ebayi, but this was considered too frivolous by the
scientific establishment. The fossil is now housed in the Natural History
Museum in London.

£1 million banknote

Issued by the UK Treasury in connection with Marshall Aid. Dated 30 August 1948, it was valid for only six weeks. The note was then given as a souvenir to the then Secretary to the Treasury, E. E. Bridges, whose signature it bears. Sold at auction by Spink of London on 1 October 2008 for £78,300.

ZWD$100 billion banknote

Introduced by Zimbabwe's central bank on 21 July 2008 in a desperate bid to ease the recurrent cash shortages plaguing the country's economy, then undergoing an official inflation rate of 2.2 million per cent. Enough to buy only four oranges, the note had an approximate value of US$1.

ZWD$100 trillion banknote

Introduced by Zimbabwe's central bank in January 2009 in response to increasing hyperinflation. Prices were doubling every day. The note had a black market value of US$33.

Jimi Hendrix's wah-wah pedal

Italian-made Vox Clyde McCoy wah-wah pedal (serial number 02683) used in the recording studio and in live concert performances by James Marshall Hendrix (born Johnny Allen Hendrix; 1942–1970). Sold by Julien's Auctions in July 2008 for $19,375.

Jack by Jackie

Untitled 10" × 8" ink on cardstock drawing by Jacqueline Kennedy.
One of eight drawings (this one depicting her husband, President
J. F. Kennedy, in a towel after a shower) all signed and dated 1961,
given by Mrs Kennedy to the seller's father, the then president of Cowles
Communications. The drawing was sold by Richard Wright of Chicago
on 1 June 2009 for $1,875, in the first auction of any works of art by the
late First Lady.

Beverly Hills Housewife by David Hockney

Oil on canvas, 1966. The 12-foot double canvas depicts Los Angeles arts patron Betty Freeman on her patio, flanked by a zebra-print Le Corbusier lounge chair, and an abstract sculpture. Sold at auction by Christie's, New York, in May 2009 for a record $7.9 million. The previous auction record for a Hockney was $5.35 million for *The Splash*, a 1966 swimming pool painting once owned by movie mogul David Geffen, sold in London by Sotheby's in 2006.

David Hockney
'Beverly Hills Housewife' 1966/67
Acrylic on 2 canvases
72" × 144"
Copyright David Hockney
Photo credit: Richard Schmidt

James Brown's lighter

Gold-plated Zippo lighter inscribed with the initials 'JB', belonging to James Joseph Brown, Jr (1933–2006), the godfather of soul. Sold at auction by Christie's on 17 July 2008 for $2,000.

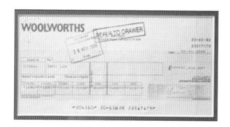

The last Woolworth's cheque

Cheque for £97,916.60 made out to Woolworth's supplier TMTI. Submitted for cashing on 26 November 2008 (the day the 99-year-old UK firm went bust), it bounced. The cheque (hopefully a good deal more legible than it appears here) made £1,080 at auction on eBay. The money was given to the National Autistic Society.

Secret MI6 tunnels

A one-mile-long atom-bomb-proof tunnel complex 100 feet below High Holborn in London. Dug in 1940, this city-under-a-city was originally designed to provide air raid accommodation for approximately 8,000 people and as a possible last-ditch base for the government in the event of an invasion. After the war, the tunnels, consisting of two main thoroughfares and four smaller offshoots (with names like South Street, Second Avenue and Tea Bar Alley, reminiscent of First World War trenches), were then requisitioned by MI6 – most notably by the 'Inter Services Research Bureau', a shady outfit that was in fact a front for the research and development arm of MI6 (perhaps better known as 'Q' branch in the James Bond novels). During the 1950s and 1960s, the site also housed the exchange for the then-famous 'hot line' that connected the leaders of Russia and the USA – the tunnels were locked down and fully manned for a fortnight during the Cuban missile crisis in 1962. Thanks to an artesian well and an independent generator (which powered old submarine chillers to keep the air breathable), staff could survive, if necessary, under the streets (and the Central Line tube) for months on end. After the end of the Cold War, the tunnels were taken over by British Telecom and the Public Records Office, but the exact details of their history remain a mystery to this day. The entrance to them (at 39 Furnival Street) remained a secret until 2009. Offered for sale by British Telecom in October 2008 for £5 million, it is thought the tunnels may be transformed into a car showroom, a shooting range or a nightclub.

Black Canary Barbie

Based on the DC Comics super-heroine of the same name, Mattel produced this doll in September 2008. Sporting fishnet stockings, PVC hotpants and black leather boots, the doll retailed in the USA for $40.

Gandhi's glasses

Steel-rimmed spectacles once belonging to Mohandas K. Gandhi.
Gandhi presented the spectacles to Colonel H. A. Shiri Diwan Nawabin
of the Indian army in the 1930s, after Nawabin had asked the great leader
for inspiration. 'They gave me the vision to free India,' the Mahatma said.
Despite attempts by the Indian government, Gandhi's family and even
the owner of the glasses, Californian documentary-maker James Otis, to
stop their sale, the auction went ahead as planned on 5 March 2009 at
Antiquorum in New York. The glasses were included in a lot (comprising
leather sandals, pocket watch, bowl and plate) that was sold for £1.27m to
Indian liquor baron Vijay Mallya.

Knights Templar chateau

Château de la Jarthe near Périgueux, in the Dordogne. Built in the twelfth century, the chateau was once a seat of the famed Christian military order, the Poor Fellow-Soldiers of Christ and of the Temple of Solomon, commonly known as the Knights Templar or the Order of the Temple. First established in 1119 by the French knight Hugues de Payens and his relative Godfrey de Saint-Omer as a force to protect Christian pilgrims from infidel attack following the First Crusade, the Order initially had few financial resources and relied on donations to survive. Their impoverishment did not last long, however. In 1139, Pope Innocent II exempted the Order from all laws in Christendom save those emanating from Rome, and the Templars grew in numbers, wealth and influence. Soldiers of incomparable bravery and skill, the Templars, in their distinctive white mantles with a red cross, were often the advance force in key battles of the Crusades. One of their most famous victories was at the Battle of Montgisard in 1177, where some 500 Templar knights helped to defeat Saladin's army of more than 26,000 soldiers. At the height of their power, the Order assumed control of a financial infrastructure never to be replicated in history: it can indeed be described as the world's first multinational. But following the re-capture of Jerusalem by Saladin's forces in 1187, the Templars' influence began to wane. Their hubristic strength had made them vulnerable, and in 1312 Pope Clement (under pressure from King Philip IV of France, who saw the chance of freeing himself from his huge debts to the Order) issued a Papal bull dissolving the order, following which many Templars were burned at the stake. But the legend of the Order as the ultimate secret elite has persisted through the centuries, not least through the medium of Dan Brown's popular fiction. Château de la Jarthe is redolent of this ancient martial romance and comprises 1,468 square metres of inside space and 120 hectares of land. It was offered for sale in June 2009 by La Perla International Living for €5,500,000.

Steve McQueen's motorcycle licence

Driver's international licence No. Z 6285. Issued to Steve McQueen by the FIM (Fédération Internationale Motocycliste). Stamped and dated 1964, the licence is signed by Steve McQueen. Together with pals Bud and Dave Ekins, Cliff Coleman and John Steen, the Hollywood star represented the USA at the 1964 International Six Day Trials. On 5 September, in a packed hall in Erfurt, East Germany, decked out with a large picture of Lenin, McQueen carried the Stars and Stripes for the US team at the opening ceremony. Sold by Bonhams on 9 May 2009 for $4,700, five times the estimate for the document.

Steve McQueen's desert racer

Replica of the bike ridden by Steve McQueen as 'Cooler King' Virgil Hilts in *The Great Escape* (1963). Built by Oxfordshire-based Metisse Motorcycles, the fully reconditioned period Triumph TR6 engine complete with a single Amal carburettor faithfully incorporates McQueen's own ideals: styled footrests (made to McQueen's original design), 35mm Ceriani forks (with seven inches of travel, which McQueen found to be the optimum), BSA yokes, Mk III chrome-moly, nickel-plated, oil-bearing frame, chromed steel wheel rims, period chromed exhausts, scramble rear tyre, trials front tyre, Amal competition levers and twist grip. A period Triumph front hub with BSA rear, along with an authentic colour-coded tank, seat and panels complete the specification. Limited to an edition of 300, each bears McQueen's signature on the tank. Available from Metisse Motorcycles for £13,999.

Ministry of Defence 'HM Forces' Action Men

First produced by Palitoy (the UK licensee for Hasbro) in 1966, the authentically styled military Action Man was for decades the staple of every British boy's toy collection. After 1993, however, Hasbro gradually reduced the figure to a sort of superannuated eco-warrior, with unlikely nemeses such as Dr X, No-Face and Professor Gangrene, before finally ceasing production in 2006. May 2009 saw the return of genuine military professionalism to the UK toy market with the issue by the MoD of a range of Action Man-style figures based on the nation's contemporary armed services. Launched on VE Day, the range includes three 10-inch replicas – infantryman, commando and pilot – each selling for £10. The MoD will get a cut of the proceeds under a licence deal with the firm Character Options. Though not sporting the original's famous fuzzy hair and eagle eyes, the figures show a keen attention to detail. The new infantry soldier figure wears exact miniatures of the desert camouflage combat clothing, boots, body armour, SA-80A2 assault rifle and Personal Role Radio employed by British troops fighting the Taliban in Afghanistan. The designers have even included the standard-issue goggles on his Kevlar ballistic protection helmet. The Royal Marine figure wears a miniature green commando beret over an appropriately steely gaze, while the RAF jet pilot carries a service pistol issued for survival behind enemy lines, a 'bone dome' flying helmet with oxygen mask, and white leather flying gloves. Replica tanks, RAF Harrier jets and remote control Royal Navy assault hovercraft will be sold alongside the figures. An MoD spokesman said: 'We are rightly proud to be celebrating our armed forces through the production of these new action figures. These toys showcase our people and equipment, and this commercial recognition proves the high level of support for our forces among the British public.'

Rommel's 'P45'

Adolf Hitler's official order removing Field Marshal Erwin Rommel from his position as Commander-in-Chief of Army Group B. Following the unsuccessful von Stauffenberg plot to assassinate the Führer at the 'Wolf's Lair' on 20 July 1944, a widespread investigation was undertaken to identify the co-conspirators. Although no evidence was found linking Rommel directly, the 'Desert Fox' was identified in some of the ringleaders' documentation as a potential supporter and an acceptable military leader to be placed in a position of responsibility should the coup succeed. The 'Court of Military Honour' (which included Heinz Guderian and Gerd von Rundstedt, two men with whom Rommel had crossed swords before) decided that Rommel should be handed over to Roland Freisler's People's Court. It was at this time – on 4 September 1944 – that this 8.5" × 11.5" document, boldly signed by Hitler himself and his Chief of Personnel, General Wilhelm Burgdorf, was issued at the Führer's headquarters. It was tantamount to Rommel's death warrant. Hitler recognised that the arrest and trial of Germany's most popular general would not sit well with the German people. Rommel was therefore approached at his home by Burgdorf and Ernst Maisel on 14 October 1944 and offered a stark choice: he could face the People's Court and potential persecution of his family, or choose to commit suicide – in which case the government would assure his family pension payments and a state funeral. After a few minutes' thought alone, Rommel announced that he would end his own life, and then explained his decision to his wife and son. Taking the phial of poison Burgdorf had brought for the occasion, Rommel returned to Burgdorf's Opel, carrying his field marshal's baton, and was driven out of the village. The driver, SS Sergeant Doose, walked away from the car, leaving Rommel with Maisel and Burgdorf. Five minutes later, Burgdorf gestured to Doose to return to the car. Doose noticed that Rommel was slumped over; sobbing, he replaced Rommel's fallen cap on the field marshal's head. Ten minutes later the group phoned Rommel's wife to inform her that her husband was dead. When Churchill heard of the field marshal's demise, he said: 'He deserves our respect, because, although a loyal German soldier, he came to hate Hitler and all his works, and took part in the conspiracy to rescue Germany by displacing the maniac and tyrant. For this, he paid the forfeit of his life. In the sombre wars of modern democracy, there is little place for chivalry.' Offered for sale by Alexander Autographs of Stamford, Connecticut, in November 2008. Estimate $40,000.

<u>Mit Wirkung vom 4.September 1944 wird versetzt:</u>

Generalfeldmarschall R o m m e l , Oberbefehlshaber der Heeresgruppe B, in die Führer-Reserve
des Oberkommandos des Heeres zu
meiner Verfügung.

<u>Mit Wirkung vom gleichen Tage werden ernannt:</u>

Generalfeldmarschall M o d e l , Oberbefehlshaber West und Oberbefehlshaber der Heeresgruppe D,
zum Oberbefehlshaber der Heeresgruppe B ,

Generalfeldmarschall von R u n d s t e d t , in der Führer-Reserve
des Oberkommandos des Heeres,
zum Oberbefehlshaber West und
Oberbefehlshaber der Heeresgruppe D.

Führerhauptquartier,den 4. September 1944

Der Führer

Der Chef
des Heeres-Personalamts
J.V.

Generalleutnant

Nr.6882/44 OKH/PA/Ag P 1/1.(Zentr.)Abt.(IIId)

007 Lotus Esprit

1976 Lotus Esprit Coupé from the 1977 film *The Spy Who Loved Me*.
One of two complete, fully functioning cars that were used in the movie.
Nine Esprits were used in different guises, but seven were shells, some of
which were used in filming the car's transformation into a submersible.
This car was used in the following scenes: where 'Q' drives off the ferry in
Sardinia and instructs Bond in its operation; where Bond (Roger Moore)
drives away with the amorous Russian agent Anya Amasova (Barbara Bach);
and where Bond is pursued by Stromberg's decorative henchwoman in a
helicopter. This is the only car that had the missile launching button on the
gear stick and the special revised housing for the clock/periscope screen.
Sold at auction by Bonhams on 1 December 2008 for £111,500.

'Jackson'

Foxhound Cross resident of Battersea Dogs Home, London.
Aged 6–12 months. Billed as 'a very intelligent youngster that
needs to learn some manners'. Offered in May 2009. Price: Free.

> feuenth day, wherefore the LORD bleſſed the Sab-
> bath day, and hallowed it.
> 12 ¶ * Honour thy father and thy mother, that
> thy dayes may bee long vpon the land which the
> LORD thy God giueth thee.
> 13 * Thou ſhalt not kill.
> 14 Thou ſhalt commit adultery.
> 15 Thou ſhalt not ſteale.
> 16 Thou ſhalt not beare falſe witneſſe againſt
> thy neighbour.
> 17 * Thou ſhalt not couet thy nighbours houſe,
> thou ſhalt not couet thy neighbours wife, nor his
> man-ſeruant, nor his maid-ſeruant, nor his oxe, nor
> his aſſe, nor any thing that is thy neighbours.

The 'Wicked' Bible

Copy of the 'Wicked' Bible. A reprint of the King James Bible,
the 'Wicked' Bible was published in 1631 in London by the royal
printers Robert Barker and Martin Lucas. The prefix 'Wicked'
(sometimes 'Adulterous', or 'Sinners'') is derived from a rather
serious mistake by the bible's compositors: the omission of the
word 'not' in the commandment 'Thou shalt not commit adultery.'
The blunder appeared in a number of copies. A year later, having
been called to the Star Chamber by King Charles I, Barker and
Lucas were fined £300 (a lifetime's wage) and deprived of their
printer's licence. Most of the copies were immediately cancelled
or burned; today only eleven survive. Offered for sale in May
2009 by Greatsite.com for $89,500.

His Holiness Pope John Paul II's 'Popemobile'

In preparation for the Holy Father's visit to Paris and Lisieux
between 30 May and 2 June 1980, the Nunciature asked Peugeot
to provide a 'reliable and discreet' vehicle as transport. A Peugeot 504
pick-up chassis was chosen by the company as a basis for the projected
vehicle. On 22 May 1980, the Peugeot design team, headed by Paul Bracq,
went hard to work on this 'spéciale podium' car. A raised platform
allowed the Pope to be clearly seen by the crowd. On his left, a small seat
was provided for Monsignor Marty, Lord Bishop of Paris. Two transparent
plastic side panels protected the Holy Father. Within three days, a 40-person
team comprising panel beaters, joiners, trimming makers, painters and
mechanics completed the car, which was finished in white upholstery
with woollen carpet. The vehicle was sold by Artcurial at Le Musée
Peugeot, Sochaux, on 14 June 2009 for €9,500, with 900km on the clock.

Hard disk of MPs' expenses

1 terabyte of data from a classified computer, containing all the expense claims made by the 646 UK Members of Parliament over the last five years. Two million documents in all, including copies of expense claim forms, handwritten comments scrawled in margins, even attached sticky notes. Offered for sale unsuccessfully by an anonymous intermediary to *The Times* on 18 March 2009 for £300,000. The intermediary was named by the *Wall Street Journal*, the *Sunday Times* and the *Mail on Sunday* as John Wick, a former major with the SAS and director of a private security company, International Security Solutions Limited. The disk was eventually sold for an undisclosed sum to the *Daily Telegraph*, in an historic scoop for the paper. The 'mole' who originally acquired the disk is still unknown.

$1 billion artwork

$1 billion artwork by Michael Marcovici. Ten million $100 banknotes stacked on twelve standard pallets. Marcovici claims it as the most expensive work of art in history. Price: presumably $1 billion.

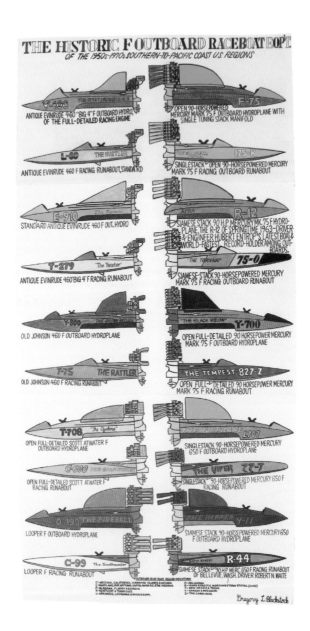

Blackstock picture

Historic F Outboard Raceboat Equip: Southern & Pacific Coasts US Regions by Gregory L. Blackstock, 2006. Ink, marker, graphite, on paper 24" × 48". Gregory Blackstock is what is known as an 'artistic savant'. His ability to render any subject of interest to him flawlessly without the use of any straight edge or formal art training is remarkable. Speaking at least 12 languages conversationally, recalling precise dates with computer-like precision and possessing an innate excellence in visual art and music, Blackstock is a rare example of this rarest category of human beings. After holding the occupation of dish steward (pot washer) for over 25 years, Blackstock is experiencing a whole new life. Now in his 60s, he is recognised as a world famous artist. This picture was offered for sale in May 2009 by the Garde Rail Gallery in Seattle for $3000.

The Panorama of the City of New York

A built-to-scale model of the city originally created for the 1964 World's Fair, the Panorama of the City of New York occupies 9,335 square feet of the old fairgrounds in Flushing Meadows Corona Park. In a novel fundraising initiative starting on 17 March 2009, the Queen's Museum of Art, the panorama's owners, introduced their 'Adopt-a-Building' programme, whereby donors will be able to purchase deeds to one of the model's 895,000 structures. Prices range from $50 for an apartment to $10,000 for a developer to install their new mega-development in the landscape.

The Corpus Clock

Sculptural clock, designed by John C. Taylor, displayed on the outside of the Taylor Library at Corpus Christi College, Cambridge. Comprising a 24-carat gold-plated stainless steel disc, about 1.5 metres in diameter, the clock has no hands or numbers but displays the time by opening individual slits in the clock face backlit with blue LEDs. These slits are arranged in three concentric rings displaying hours (inner ring), minutes (middle ring) and seconds (outer ring). The clock's clockwork is entirely mechanically controlled, without any computer programming, and electricity is used only for a motor which winds up the mechanism and powers the blue LEDs. The dominating feature of the clock is a particularly sinister-looking grasshopper escapement atop the dial which appears to hungrily devour the seconds. A homage to John Harrison's original eighteenth-century grasshopper escapement, Taylor calls this his 'Chronophage' (literally 'time eater' in Greek). At apparently irregular intervals, the pendulum stops and the grasshopper moves its mouth and blinks its eyes as if in smug contemplation of the fact that for us humans time is inexorably running out. Below the clock is an inscription from the Vulgate 1 John 2:17: *mundus transit et concupiscentia eius* ('the world passeth away, and the lust thereof'). Taylor invested five years in the Corpus Clock project, which involved 200 people, including engineers, sculptors, scientists, jewellers and calligraphers. The clockwork incorporates six new patented inventions. It was officially unveiled to the public on 19 September 2008 by Cambridge physicist Stephen Hawking. John C. Taylor will now be undertaking limited and exclusive commissions for the 'Chronophage', each one customised for the client, which he expects to retail at upwards of £1 million.

Uncle Monty's cottage

'Very cheap to those who can afford it. Very expensive to those who can't,' as Withnail himself has it, having secured the keys from his bibulous relative. Derelict 1802 farmhouse (Sleddale Hall) near Shap in Cumbria, rented as a location for the 1984 film *Withnail and I*. Sold without planning permission at auction on 17 February 2009 for £265,000. The successful bidder, a local pub boss, intends to restore it as a place of pilgrimage for fans of the film.

Your complete human genome

The genome, a map of all the DNA in the human body, serves
as a blueprint for an individual's physical and behavioural traits
as well as their susceptibility to diseases. Ever since the first human
genome sequence was completed in 2003, there have been hopes that
genome sequencing will help usher in a new era of individualised
healthcare. On 25 April 2009, in honour of DNA Day, Massachusetts-based
Knome and the non-profit X Prize Foundation offered a complete human
genome sequencing package to the winner of a ten-day auction on eBay.
The package was sold to an unknown European for $68,000.

The real Mr Darcy

Miniature portrait by George Engleheart (1776–1868) of Tom Langlois Lefroy, 1798. Jane Austen expended little energy on the physical description of her characters in *Pride and Prejudice*. She goes only as far as conveying, through the mouths of several in the book, that Darcy is 'tall' and 'handsome'. To a modern audience, the appearance of Austen's hero has been inextricably linked to hunky types like Matthew McFadden and Colin Firth. But how did the author really imagine the master of Pemberley? The only visual clue in existence lies in this picture of a young Irish lawyer named Tom Lefroy. Austen first met Lefroy in December 1795 at a ball at Manydown House in Hampshire when they were both twenty. They both quickly found themselves in love. Their union was tragically thwarted, however, by the question of money. Lefroy's father, a lieutenant-colonel of moderate means, insisted that his eldest son (having five sisters) must marry a rich woman. Jane, alas, also from a large family with few resources, had only her writing to provide her with an income. They met for the last time – again at a ball – at Ashe Rectory, Hampshire, in January 1796. Having risen to the post of Lord Chief Justice of Ireland in 1852 (and having married an heiress in 1799), Lefroy, as a very old man, acknowledged when questioned that he had loved Jane Austen in 1796. It is generally accepted that he formed the basis for Austen's great literary creation. Signed with Engleheart's distinctive cursive 'E', the picture is offered for sale by Judy and Brian Harden for £50,000.

Dylan's mouth organ

Hohner Marine Band (B) harmonica. Used and signed by Bob Dylan
in black marker. Sold by SamAshMusic.com in October 2008 for $25,000.

Kennedy car, Dallas, 22 November 1963

Scale 1:43 die-cast 1961 Lincoln X-100. For sale from Minichamps for £44.99.

Luke Skywalker's lightsabre

Used by Mark Hamill as Luke Skywalker in both *Star Wars* (1977)
and *The Empire Strikes Back* (1980). Constructed from a Graflex
flashgun from the 1930s. Offered for sale by Gary Kurtz, producer
of the two films, this instrument of 'the force' was sold at auction
on 12 December 2008 by Profiles in History in Los Angeles for $207,743.

'Force' trainer

Mind-control toy (created in 2009 by US Uncle Milton Industries) designed to test and hone your Jedi skills. The toy comes with a sensor headset which measures the extent of the wearer's brain activity which is then, via circuitry, translated into physical action – in this case moving a ball up a tube. The deeper the level of the wearer's concentration, the further up the tube the ball will go. The toy is based on EEG (electroencephalography) technology, which records electrical activity along the scalp produced by the firing of neurons within the brain. Star Wars sound effects and audio clips emitted from the base unit cue you in to progress from Padawan to Jedi. To be universally retailed in the USA from 2009 for $100.

Bobby Fischer's library

Personal collection of the genius of chess. Comprising over 300 chess books in various languages, approximately 400 issues of chess-related periodicals, nine personal floppy disks (unexamined), three sets of proofs for Fischer's *My 60 Memorable Games* (published in 1969), four volumes of bound typescript detailing the match history of Boris Spassky from the 1950s to 1971, and fifteen volumes of ring- or string-bound manuscript notebooks with notation of the games of Mark Taimanov and Tigran Petrossian from the 1950s to 1970.

The manuscript material centres on Fischer's preparation for his historic match with Boris Spassky. On 11 July 1972, with a presidential crisis stirring in the USA and the Cold War at a pivotal point, Boris Vasilievich Spassky, the (refreshingly un-Soviet) Soviet World Chess Champion, and Robert J. Fischer, his American challenger, sat down opposite each other in a Reykjavik sports hall to contest what was to be the most documented and notorious chess match of all time. Over the next two months, Spassky, a chess-playing machine who had returned the title to the Kremlin for years, and Fischer, a 29-year-old goofy and egocentric loner from Brooklyn, riveted the chess-playing and non-chess-playing world as they vied not only for the ultimate prize in chess but for intellectual hegemony of their respective political systems. Fischer's win in 'The Match of the Century' ended 24 years of Soviet domination of the world championship and was viewed with elation by the western world. Described as the 'Codex Leicester of Chess', this documentary record of one of the outstanding brains in history was sold by Bonhams on 10 June 2009 for $61,000.

Rare bead necklace by Marcel Wanders

Designed by the Dutch artist in 2008. Produced in a limited
edition of only 30, the necklace comprises:

A Baccarat bead (replica of a bead from a chandelier made for the
    Russian Tsar Nicolai II).
A golden 'Wanders Wonders' bead.
A black pearl.
A gallbladder stone.
A time bead (a gold bead painted white that turns gold with wearing).
A Niessing steel bead.
A hand-painted porcelain bead.
A replica of a bead from Queen Elizabeth II's rattle.
A miniature ping pong ball bead.
A Swarovski bead.
A knot bead (referring to Wanders's 1995 *Knotted Chair*).
A one-minute bead (handmade in one minute).
A lava bead.
A shooting star bead (meteorite particle).
An African fertility bead.
An origami bead.
A 10mg Viagra pill.

Offered for sale by 20ltd.com for £2,000.

Enigma cipher machine

A ten-rotor Enigma cipher machine manufactured as the 'Secret Writer T 52c' in 1935 by the German company Siemens & Halske AG. An electro-mechanical device using a series of rotating 'wheels' or 'rotors' to scramble plain text messages into incoherent cipher text, the Enigma machine was used extensively by the German authorities to encode secret messages during World War Two. As it was capable of being set to billions of combinations, the Germans were confident of the machine's invulnerability to decryption. The machine did however have a weakness: enciphered German transmissions often contained common words or phrases (e.g. the names of generals, weather reports, etc.). This enabled Allied codebreakers to make informed guesses at the meaning of short fragments of the original message and, using these 'cribs', mathematicians working at Bletchley Park (most notably Alan Turing and Gordon Welchman) succeeded in cracking the Enigma code in early 1940. The value of this intelligence (codenamed 'Ultra') has long been debated, but it is generally accepted that it shortened the war by as much as two years. Offered for sale in May 2009 by Breker.com for €50,000.

A pot of M. Dutriez's Bar-Le-Duc redcurrant jam

Bar-le-Duc in north-east France has been making fine jams and preserves for the last 700 years. Until the French Revolution there were hundreds of jam makers in Bar-le-Duc, producing up to 100,000lb of jam every year. Over the centuries, however, the number of producers has dwindled to just a handful – indeed, M. Dutriez purchased the last remaining maker of the region's unique redcurrant jam in 1974. Since 1344, the key to the fame of Bar-le-Duc's jam has been in the deseeding of the fruit, a process undertaken by hand and using quills from goose feathers. The smoothness of the jam is still achieved in the same way today. M. Dutriez's épépineuses (seed-removers) work at home during three weeks in June every year and are paid by the weight of seedless redcurrants they deliver. An experienced épépineuse can produce 1kg of deseeded fruits in three hours. A favourite of many from Mary, Queen of Scots to Alfred Hitchcock, a tiny pot of Bar-le-Duc jam today costs around €15.

Obama's Illinois senate seat

Illinois senate seat, vacated by Barack Obama, allegedly offered for
sale to the 'highest bidder' by Illinois Governor Rod Blagojevich. Following
the results of an investigation by the FBI using wiretaps and listening
devices planted in the Serb-American Governor's office (including the
recorded words: 'I've got this thing and it's f***ing golden, and uh, uh, I'm
just not giving it up for f***in' nothing'), Blagojevich and his chief of staff,
John Harris, appeared in a Chicago federal courthouse on 9 December
2008 to answer charges of conspiracy to commit mail and wire fraud
and solicitation of bribery. In January 2009, senators voted 59–0 to
remove Blagojevich from the governorship, replacing him with his
former running mate and lieutenant governor, Patrick Quinn, who
was sworn in as the state's 41st governor. Patrick Fitzgerald, US Attorney
for Northern Illinois, said that Blagojevich's 'conduct would make Lincoln
roll over in his grave', but that the case 'makes no allegations about
[President Obama] whatsoever'. Newly-elected President Obama
commented: 'I had no contact with the governor or his office, and
so I was not aware of what was happening. It is a sad day for Illinois.
Beyond that I don't think it's appropriate to comment.'

W. G. Grace's bat

Full size Cobbett cricket bat as used by W. G. Grace over two or
more seasons, culminating in the 1896 Ashes series, when he scored
his 1,000th run in tests during the first test. Fully corded grip and
double cording to the body of the bat by the cricketer. Signed to
the front face 'England v Australia June 1896', with the autographs
of the following England greats beneath: Lyttleton, W. G. Grace,
Hayward, Stoddart, Lilley, Barlow, Hearne, E. M. Grace, Capt.
A. W. Webbe, and others. Also signed by the Australian 'Demon'
bowler, Fred Spofforth, and to the bottom of the front face by Lloyd
George. Offered for sale in June 2009 at Britishsportsmuseum.com
for £20,000.

MENU

Fruit Juices

Chilled Quartered Oranges
with Grape Fruit

Cereals with Fresh Cream

Fresh Eggs *POACH* × 1st course
(Boiled, Scrambled, Fried in Butter)

Grilled Bacon . Tomatoes
Mushrooms . Chipolatas

1st ——

Toast ~~Melba~~
White and Wholemeal Bread
Fancy Rolls   ,st ——
Fresh Farm Butter
Oxford Marmalade   1st ——
JAM

Indian ~~and China Tea~~
Coffee   1st course
Cold Milk *give jug with coffee*
         as well as hot
Basket of Fresh Fruit   *milk*

Churchill's in-flight 'whisky' breakfast

Menu for breakfast written by Winston Churchill during his last
flight to the USA as prime minister. On the BOAC flight in June
1954, the standard menu offered by the plane's staff proved inadequate
for the 79-year-old premier. At first he tried to amend the printed menu,
but in the end wrote out his own on the other side. He requested his meal
to be brought on two trays. The first tray included: poached egg, toast,
jam, butter, coffee, milk, cold milk jug, cold chicken or meat. The second
tray included: grapefruit, sugar bowl, glass of orange squash (with ice),
a whisky soda and a cigar. Sold at auction on 23 April 2009 by Mullocks
Auctioneers in Ludlow for £5,600.

General Gordon's secret message

Having been instructed by the British government to oversee withdrawal from the Sudan in the face of the Mahdi uprising, Major-General Charles George Gordon (1833–1885) marched into Khartoum on 18 February 1884. But no sooner had he started evacuating women, children and the wounded back to Egypt, than the Mahdi's forces closed in on the city. From 18 March Khartoum was under siege. This postage stamp-sized secret message, written in Gordon's hand and smuggled out concealed in a courier's hair, shows Gordon's confidence that relief was on its way. Written in Arabic, it translates as: 'Mudir of Dongola Khartoum and Senaar in perfect security. Mahamed Ahmed carries this to give you news. On his reaching you, give him all the news as to the direction & position of the relieving force and their numbers. As for Khartoum there are in it 8,000 men and the Nile is rapidly rising. On arrival of the bearer give him 100 reals mejide'h from the States. (signed) C. G. Gordon.' But a British force under General Sir Gerald Graham, despite being within striking distance of Khartoum, was ordered to withdraw by Prime Minister William Gladstone, and it was not until 28 January 1885 that the Gordon Relief Expedition finally reached Khartoum. They found the city captured and Gordon dead and decapitated. The uncertain manner of Gordon's death has been romanticised in art by George William Joy's painting *General Gordon's Last Stand*, and in the film *Khartoum* (1966), with Charlton Heston in the leading role. Sold by Mullocks Auctioneers in Ludlow on 29 January 2009 for £1,150.

'Original' Levi's

Pair of 1890s Levi Strauss 201 jeans (authenticated by Lynn Downey, brand historian at Levi's) found in a miner's cabin in Montana, complete with the original dirt, wax, spider webs, splinters and gold dust. Sold on eBay in July 2008 for $36,099.

Château Latour

Château Latour in Bordeaux. The vineyard comprises 78 hectares in all, but only grapes from the 47 hectares (known as L'Enclos) that directly surround the chateau go into the eponymous first wine. Owned since 1993 by French business tycoon François H. Pinault, the vineyard was reported to be for sale in December 2008. While the *Sunday Times* cited a potential price tag of €150–€200m, sources in Bordeaux suggested that the property would not go for less than €600m.

Super Lemon Haze

Super Lemon Haze marijuana. Winner of the 2008 High Times Cannabis Cup (held in Amsterdam from 23 to 28 November) with a landslide vote. Cited for its 'sharp and intense aroma reminiscent of lemon, lime and pink grapefruit', followed by a 'very earthy and musky haze aftertaste, with traces of incense and black pepper'. THC (Tetrahydrocannabinol): 22.9%. 'Induces a finely balanced physical/cerebral high.' Price: Street value.

Bill With Shark **by Damien Hirst**

Oil painting based on a photograph by Jean Pigozzi depicting Bill Gates looking at Hirst's *The Physical Impossibility of Death in the Mind of Someone Living*. Sold at auction on 16 September 2008 at Sotheby's, on behalf of the Bill and Melinda Gates Foundation, for £313,250.

Mr Chu's dog collar

One of five dog collars worn by pugs belonging to the Duke and Duchess of Windsor. The Duke (Edward VIII) and Duchess (Mrs Simpson) were particular fans of pugs. They reportedly fed them from F. B. Rogers silver dog bowls and scented them with Miss Dior, Wallis Simpson's favourite fragrance. One animal, named Diamond, used to sleep on the Duke's bed, but ran away and only returned on the night of his death. Which of their eleven pugs – among them Mr Chu, Dizzy (after Disraeli), Davy Crockett, Impy, Rufus, Gen Sengh, Winston, Minoru and Trooper – actually sported this collar is unknown. All the same, it is unequivocally inscribed 'I belong to the Duke of Windsor'. Offered for sale in a lot of five collars by Bonhams in February 2009 for $3,000.

Gatsby's Rolls

1928 Rolls-Royce 40/50hp Phantom I Ascot Dual Cowl Sports Phaeton with coachwork by Brewster, used in the 1974 film of *The Great Gatsby*. Owned by Massachusetts collector Ted Leonard, who lent it for the film, the car was carefully adapted to adhere to F. Scott Fitzgerald's description in the original 1925 novel: 'It was a rich cream color, bright with nickel, swollen here and there in its monstrous length with triumphant hat-boxes and supper-boxes and tool-boxes, and terraced with a labyrinth of wind-shields that mirrored a dozen suns.' Later in the story, the old-money character Tom Buchanan describes the car as a 'circus wagon'. Sold at auction by Bonhams during the Greenwich Concours d'Elégance in Connecticut in June 2009 for $238,000.

A B C D E F G H I J K L M
N O P Q R S T U V W X Y Z

a b c d e f g h i j k l m
n o p q r s t u v w x y z

1 2 3 4 5 6 7 8 9 0

Baskerville 10

Typeface created in 2008 in collaboration with Czech designer Otakar
Karlas by the Dutchman František Štorm. Baskerville 10 is a set of four
OpenType fonts with pan-European Latin, Cyrillic and Greek alphabets.
Storm admires Baskerville's letter for its 'sober elegance and clear design'
and attests to its 'character of a gentleman'. While this respect for the
English master is clearly visible in his adaptation, Storm by no means
slavishly followed the historical specimens. Rather he created 'a beautiful,
lively and very practical text family for all sorts of text work'. This book
is typeset in Baskerville 10. The Baskerville 10 Pro family, containing
8 fonts, is available from Stormtype.com for €190.

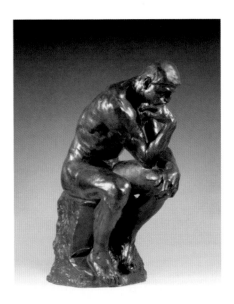

Rodin's *The Thinker*

Bronze sculpture (72.5cm high) by François-Auguste-René Rodin (1840–1917). One of 21 *The Thinker* sculptures made by Rodin in the late nineteenth century and early twentieth century. Originally named *The Poet*, the piece was designed to be part of Rodin's monumental *Gates of Hell* (commissioned by the Musée des Arts Décoratifs in 1880), inspired by Dante's *Divine Comedy*. Sold at auction in June 2009 by Drouot of Paris for $5.2 million – a record for *The Thinker* sculptures sold to date.

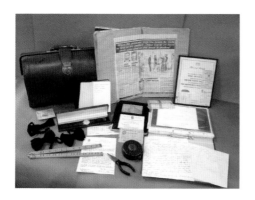

The personal collection of Britain's last hangman

The diary and tools of the trade of Harry Bernard Allen (1911–1992), Britain's last executioner, who officiated at the gallows between 1941 and 1964. Allen was chief executioner at 29 executions and assistant (mostly to Albert Pierrepoint) at 53 others. Allen performed the last execution in Northern Ireland when he hanged Robert McGladden in 1961; the last execution in Scotland when he hanged Henry Burnett in 1963; and one of the two final executions in England when he hanged Gwynne Owen Evans at Strangeways, Manchester, in 1964. One of Allen's most controversial executions was of James Hanratty in 1962. Hanratty was convicted of the murder on 22 August 1961 of Michael Gregsten at Deadman's Hill on the A6, near the village of Clophill, Bedfordshire. A cause célèbre for opponents of the death penalty, much energy has been devoted over the years (including documentaries on Channel 4 and the BBC) to casting doubt on the validity of this conviction. Modern testing of DNA from Hanratty's exhumed corpse convinced Court of Appeal judges in 2002 that his guilt was proved 'beyond doubt', although Paul Foot and other campaigners continue to believe in Hanratty's innocence. Harry Allen's main occupation was as a lorry driver and later a publican in the Manchester area. His hobbies included bowling. He died in 1992. The collection, sold by his wife at auction through Frank Marshall & Co., Cheshire, in October 2008 for £17,200, included Allen's execution diary (containing handwritten lists of his executions, with details of the condemned prisoner's name, date of execution, age, height, weight and drop, etc. – some with remarks including 'the last words of the condemned prisoner') and the black bow ties Allen wore on execution days as a sign of respect.

Oscar Wilde's cane

Ivory-handled cane belonging to Oscar Fingal O'Flahertie Wills Wilde (1854–1900). The cane is inscribed with the letters 'OW, C33', Wilde's initials and cell location in Reading Gaol (Block C, Floor 3, Cell 3), where he was imprisoned for two years after being convicted of gross indecency on 25 May 1895. Prison was unkind to Wilde's health, and after he was released on 19 May 1897 he spent his last three years in Paris, where he died on 30 November 1900, in penniless, self-imposed exile from society and artistic circles. Valued pre-sale at £500, the cane, part of a lot that also included his brass inkwell, was sold at auction by Lyon and Turnbull in Edinburgh in March 2009 for £7,725.

Drawing of a seven-legged spider by David Thorne

Felt-tip on paper, 2008. The global viral fame of the drawing of the
seven-legged spider emanated from the email correspondence alleged
to have been exchanged between a Mr David Thorne and a Ms Jane
Gilles. Mr Thorne, having been contacted by Ms Gilles with a request
that he pay the $233.95 outstanding on his phone bill, replied to Ms
Gilles that he unfortunately had no money but that he hoped she would
accept his picture of a spider that, in his personal calculation, had
a current market value of $233.95. Ms Gilles then cordially responded
that the company did not accept drawings in lieu of payment and that
he should pay the outstanding amount forthwith. Mr Thorne then
emailed to say in that case could he have his spider back. A little frustrated
and confused, Ms Gilles duly emailed back the picture. Mr Thorne then
noticed that the spider in the picture only had seven legs and emailed
Ms Gilles to say that she had sent him the wrong picture as he refused
to believe he had neglected to attach the correct number of limbs. The
correspondence continued... The original drawing was then sold on
eBay in October 2008 for a reported $15,000.

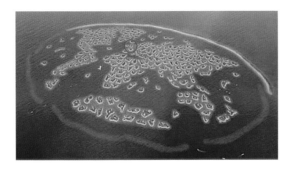

'Great Britain'

The 'Great Britain' island in the real estate company Nakheel's offshore development epic 'The World' in Dubai. Two British men bought the 11-acre man-made island for £40 million in January 2009. Safi Qurashi and Mustafa Nagri announced plans to recreate the architecture of their homeland in the Gulf and hope to begin building on it next year.

Lamborghini police car

Lamborghini Gallardo LP560–4 issued to the Italian police in October 2008. Powered by a 560 horsepower engine and capable of speeds up to 203mph, the car will be based in the Lazio region and stalk the autostradas around Rome. It will be driven by a roster of 30 specifically trained officers and comes equipped with a specially designed mini fridge used to transport organs and plasma to help save the lives of traffic accident victims. Price: £140,000.

SS *United States*

990-foot-long ocean liner acknowledged as the nation's flagship
– built by William Francis Gibbs's company Gibbs & Cox (1950–1952).
Immediately after World War Two, General John M. Franklin, President of
the United States Lines, approached William Francis Gibbs, designer of 70
per cent of all US wartime naval vessels, and asked him to design the finest
ship American industry, ingenuity, and skill could build. In order to get a
crucial government subsidy for the proposed $70 million vessel, she also
had to be a military asset. By 1949, Gibbs had unveiled plans for a ship that
could, within one week, be converted into a troop carrier for 14,000 troops
and could steam non-stop at 33 knots for 10,000 miles without refuelling.
Construction started in early 1950 at the Newport News Shipbuilding and
Dry Dock Company, and the ship was ready to receive passengers in July
1952. On 7 July 1952, the SS *United States* seized the Atlantic speed record
from Britain's *Queen Mary*, travelling the 3,000 miles between New York and
England in a mere 3 days, 10 hours and 40 minutes, averaging just under
36 knots. As America's 'First Lady of the Seas', the ship became an instant
sensation with the American public. Models, toys, advertisements and
posters proliferated throughout the nation. Progress, however, was not on
her side. In 1969, the SS *United States* succumbed to airline competition,
labour strife and the withdrawal of government operating subsidies, and
was taken out of service. After four decades of neglect, mutilation, and failed
revitalisation schemes, this largely-forgotten icon of American technology
and power now languishes on Columbus Boulevard in Philadelphia. In
February 2009, Norwegian Cruise Lines/Star Cruises, the ship's Hong Kong-
based owner, were, despite protests by the SS *United States* Conservancy
Board, preparing to sell America's national flagship to the highest bidder.

Smog-eating cement

In response to American architect Richard Meier's requirement for
a very white material for his Jubilee Church in Rome in 2003, the Italian
company Italcementi developed a special cement using titanium dioxide
(traditionally used to whiten paint). It did the job extremely well. It
wasn't until years later, however, that so-called 'TX Active' was discovered
to have another exciting property. The cement's titanium dioxide
component was found, under the right conditions, to neutralise harmful
pollutants. 'When exposed to sunlight or ultraviolet light, the titanium
dioxide is activated,' explained Enrico Borgarello, Italcementi's head of
research and development, 'and pollutants that come in contact with the
surface of the cement are oxidised. Hazardous nitrogen oxides and
sulphur oxides, for example, are transformed into harmless nitrates or
sulphates, which simply rinse off the building with rainwater. This also
keeps it especially clean.' As a demonstration of TX Active's smog-
busting potential, a stretch of road in downtown Bergamo (where
Italcementi is based) was coated with a layer of the special substance.
Borgarello maintained that residents reported better-smelling air within
4.5 square miles. The company said that their research showed that if
15 per cent of the surface area of Milan were covered in TX Active, air
pollution in the city would be reduced by 50 per cent. TX Active is
sold for around £450 per tonne compared to conventional cement's
£350 per tonne.

*Pictured: Jubilee Church in Rome by Richard Meier, constructed
with TX Active. Photographs copyright Andrea Jemolo*

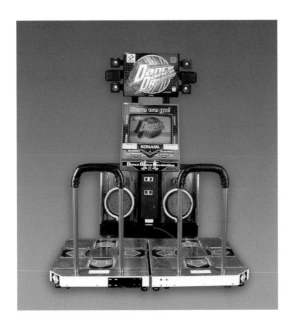

Michael Jackson's Dance Dance Revolution Arcade Game

From the personal collection of Michael Joseph Jackson (1958–2009).
1992 arcade game (serial number 845202229) offered for sale by Julien's
Auctions of West Hollywood, California, two days after the superstar's
death on 25 June 2009. Estimate: $1,000–$1,500. Introduced by Konami
in 1998, Dance Dance Revolution was a pioneer of the rhythm and dance
genre in video games. Players stand on a 'dance platform' and hit coloured
arrows laid out in a cross with their feet to musical and visual cues. Players
are judged by how well they time their dance to the patterns presented to
them. The owner of this particular machine was presumably in the habit of
winning this game.

Dean Martin's tux

Dinner suit owned and worn by Dean Martin (born Dino Paul
Crocetti; 1917–1995). Sold by Julien's Auctions in July 2008 for $20,000.

Air Jordan 4 (IV) UNDEFEATED trainers

Designed by UNDEFEATED's own Eddie Cruz and inspired by the
MA-1 flight jacket, the olive, oiled suede and flight satin UNDEFEATED Air
Jordan 4s remain the rarest and most sought-after Air Jordan 4s of all time.
Only 72 pairs were made, and these were only made available through an
auction and raffle held simultaneously from 23 June 2005. Offered for sale
on eBay in June 2009 for $7,500.

Captain Cook's boomerang

Wooden Aboriginal weapon acquired by Captain James Cook on
his first voyage to Australia in 1770. Cook became the first European
to reach and survey the eastern coast of Australia. Joseph Banks,
a botanist on Cook's ship, the *Endeavour*, described the resident
Aboriginals as 'a very pusillanimous people' who brandished a 'wooden
weapon made something like a short scymetar'. According to the Oxford
English Dictionary, the word 'boomerang' derived in the early nineteenth
century from the native Australian words 'bumarin' and 'wo-mur-rang'.
The property of a descendant of John Leach Bennett, a beneficiary of
the will of Captain Cook's widow Elizabeth, the weapon (together with
two clubs also belonging to the explorer) was offered for sale at auction
by Christie's on 25 September 2008 with an estimate of $40,000–$60,000.
(In the period leading up to the sale, concern was raised as to the
authenticity of the piece. Though this concern was slight and based
on no new information, Christie's decided of course to withdraw it
from the September sale until further research could be conducted.)

Photograph of Jonathan the tortoise

Photograph (circa 1900) showing adult male tortoise munching grass with a Boer War prisoner on St Helena. The tortoise, from the species *Testudinipae Cytodira*, is claimed to have already been 50 years old when he first arrived on the island from the Seychelles in 1882. Tortoise experts say that the photograph (recently discovered in the collection of Boer War images taken by L. A. Innes, who had a studio in St Helena's capital, Jamestown) authenticates this claim, making Jonathan, who is still alive today, at least 177 years old, and the world's oldest living animal. Today Jonathan lives in the grounds of Plantation House, the governor of St Helena's residence, with fellow land tortoises David, Speedy, Emma, Fredricka and Myrtle, and is said to mate valiantly and regularly with the three females. The photograph was sold by Andrew Smith Auctioneers of Itchen Stoke, near Winchester, in November 2008 for £4,000.

Picture (bottom): Jonathan today

The Kauffmann House

1946 five-bedroom, five-bathroom vacation house in Palm Springs. Commissioned by Edgar J. Kauffmann Sr, a Pittsburgh department store tycoon, and designed by Richard Neutra (1892–1970), the architect responsible for bringing the International Style to America. Described as the most important domestic residence in the USA today, it is offered for sale by Crosby Doe Associates of Beverly Hills for $12.95m.

Copyright Roman Salicki

Pamela Anderson's swimsuit

Red Lycra one-piece worn by the *Baywatch* actress in the 1990s show. Signed 'Love Pamela Lee, XO', it was offered for sale at auction by Profiles in History in Los Angeles in June 2009. Estimate: $2,000–$3,000.

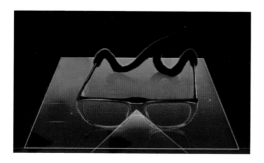

X-ray glasses

'X-Reflec' X-ray specs. Created by Bangkok-based company Advanced Intelligence, the glasses use infrared technology to permit their wearer to see through 70 per cent of clothing fibres. A particularly clear result is apparently achieved when looking at swimwear. Etailed by Advanced Intelligence for $2,400, the glasses come complete with cables that plug into the Palm Size Portable DVR so that, in 470 lines of resolution, your day's viewing can be reprised at leisure.

Smoking Hepburn stamp

€0.56 stamp depicting Audrey Hepburn smoking a cigarette in her role as Holly Golightly in the 1961 film *Breakfast at Tiffany's*. In 2001, the German government printed 14 million of the stamps as part of a series featuring film stars including Charlie Chaplin, Marilyn Monroe and Greta Garbo. The whole print run was later incinerated after Hepburn's son, Sean Ferrer, objected to the cigarette holder dangling from the actress's mouth. The Finance Ministry, however, had already delivered advance copies to the German post office for approval. Thirty of these proof copies escaped destruction when an unknown employee pocketed them and used them to send letters postmarked from Berlin. 'We can only guess that whoever took the Hepburn stamps from Deutsche Post didn't realise their value, thought they would save 56 cents and just used them on normal letters,' said Andreas Schlegel, the auctioneer. Thought to be the only one of the thirty to survive, the stamp was sold at auction on 27 May 2009 by Schlegel in Berlin for €53,500. Mr Ferrer said he hoped the anonymous seller would use proceeds from the auction to support cancer research or anti-smoking campaigns. His mother had died of colon cancer in 1993.

Honda Super Cub special 50th anniversary edition

In 1958, Honda attempted to break into the lucrative 2-stroke-dominated motorbike market with a 4-stroke machine. The result was the Honda Super Cub. Since then, over 60 million of the machines have been sold – a statistic that by an almost unbelievable margin makes it the best-selling powered vehicle of all time, the runners up being as follows: the Toyota Corolla (35m sales), the Ford F-series (30m sales), the VW Golf (25m sales), the VW Beetle (22.5m sales) and the Ford Escort (20m sales). In celebration of this unique automotive achievement, Honda created this special 50th anniversary edition. Offered for sale in July 2008 for $1,905.

Ulysses, first edition

First edition of _Ulysses_ by James Joyce. Copy number 45, of the first 100. Printed on fine Dutch handmade paper. Signed by the author. Hailed by some as the greatest novel ever written, _Ulysses_ was uncertainly received when first published in 1922. One reviewer complained that it 'appears to have been written by a perverted lunatic who has made a speciality of the literature of the latrine'. The book chronicles the passage of Leopold Bloom through Dublin during an ordinary day, 16 June 1904, and is divided into eighteen episodes – the notoriously racy last of which contains Molly Bloom's soliloquy, ending in her orgasmic 'yes I said yes I will Yes'. This near-pristine first edition is unopened apart from this last episode, which has been keenly thumbed. Banned in the UK and the USA during the 1920s, this ultra-rare copy, one of only four of the original 100 unaccounted for, was bought by a Mrs Hewitt Morgan at the subversive Manhattan bookshop _Sunwise Turn_. It remained in the Morgan family, stored in its original box, before being sold by Pom Harrington at the Antiquarian Book Fair, Olympia, London, on 4 June 2009 for £275,000, the highest price recorded for a twentieth-century first edition.

First Superman comic

June 1938 copy of *Action Comics* featuring the first appearance of the
superhero ('The Man of Steel', 'The Man of Tomorrow', 'The Last
Son of Krypton') originally created by American writer Jerry Siegel
and Canadian-born artist Joe Shuster in 1932. Sold for 10 cents when
first published, it is one of only 100 copies now remaining. Stephen
Fishler, the co-owner with Vincent Zurzolo of the online auction site
Comic Connect, said the comic had been in the same hands since
1950, when a young boy on the US west coast bought it for 35 cents.
Sold at online auction by Comic Connect of New York in March
2009 for $317,200.

The last picture of Marilyn Monroe

1962 photograph of Marilyn Monroe and jazz pianist Buddy Greco.
Taken by Greco's assistant during a weekend break (also attended
by Frank Sinatra and Bobby Kennedy's brother-in-law, Peter Lawford)
at Lake Tahoe, Nevada, it is the last image of Monroe alive. Five days
later, on 5 August, Sergeant Jack Clemmons of the LAPD received a call
at 4.25 am from Dr Ralph Greenson, Monroe's psychiatrist, announcing
that she was dead at her home in Brentwood, Los Angeles, California.
The official cause of death was classified at the time by Dr Thomas Noguchi
of the Los Angeles County Coroner's office as 'acute barbiturate poisoning',
which he recorded as an accidental overdose. Controversy still persists
around the timing and circumstances of her death. Much ink and celluloid
have been expended over the decades in promoting the idea that Monroe
was the victim of a murder conspiracy involving Peter Lawford, designed
to cover up her affairs with the Kennedy brothers. There seems, however,
to be little evidence for this. The reported facts remain that at 7.15 pm on the
night of 4 August Marilyn received a phone call from Joe DiMaggio, during
which she was declared to be 'happy' and 'in good spirits', and
that at 7.45 she received a second call, this time from Peter Lawford,
who testified that Monroe's voice was by then slurred and inaudible:
'Say goodbye to the President, and say goodbye to yourself,' she said.
What exactly transpired during those thirty minutes may never be known.
The most likely theory, expounded by Donald Spoto in his 1993 biography,
seems to be that, on medical instructions, Marilyn's housekeeper Eunice
Murray unwittingly administered an overdose enema – a procedure for
which she was untrained – to Marilyn, from which she failed to regain
consciousness. The last photograph of Marilyn Monroe was offered
for sale by Buddy Greco by online auction in June 2009 with a starting
bid of $7,500.

The last picture of Florence Nightingale

1910 photograph of Florence Nightingale (1820–1910), taken shortly before her death. Taken by Lizzie Caswall Smith, this rare image (particularly so since Nightingale intensely disliked being photographed) shows the nursing heroine of the Crimea in the bedroom of her home in South Street, just off London's Park Lane, aged 90. After the Crimean War (during which she became famously known as 'The Lady with the Lamp'), Florence set up the Nightingale Training School and Home for Nurses based at St Thomas's Hospital in London. For much of her life, Florence Nightingale was bedridden due to an illness that she contracted in the Crimea, which prevented her from nursing. In 1883 Queen Victoria awarded her the Royal Red Cross for her work, and in 1907 she became the first woman to receive the Order of Merit from Edward VII. Sold by Dreweatts of Newbury on 19 November 2008 for £5,500.

Fleet Foxes by Fleet Foxes

Full-length debut album by Fleet Foxes. Released July 2008 on the Bella Union label. Retailed by HMV.com for £8.99.

Unnamed pure-bred female camel

Bought in September 2008 by the Crown Prince of Dubai, Sheikh Hamdan bin Mohammed bin Rashed Al-Maktoum, at the Mazayin Dhafra Camel Festival in Abu Dhabi for 9.9 million dirhams (£1.8 million). The most expensive – and presumably the fastest – camel in history.

Frank Sinatra's house

Twin Palms, the original desert home (from 1947 to 1954) of Frank Sinatra, designed as his first commission by E. Stewart William. Scene of Hollywood glamour at its zenith and backdrop to Sinatra's tempestuous second marriage to Ava Gardner (one of the bathroom basins in the house still bears a crack sustained by a champagne bottle thrown at Gardner by Sinatra), the house established Palm Springs as a refuge for LA film royalty and architectural modernism. The 4,500 sq ft four-bedroom house, complete with piano-shaped swimming pool, is offered for sale by Crosby Doe Associates of Beverly Hills for $3,250,000.

Sir Peter Viggers's duck house

Stockholm duck house for which the Tory MP for Gosport claimed £1,645 on expenses. Sir Peter, who is to stand down at the next election, announced on 8 June 2009 his intention to sell the duck house for charity in due course. Adam Partridge, auctioneer from TV's *Flog It*, *Bargain Hunt* and *Cash in the Attic*, said he believed the duck house could sell for much more than its normal value of about £300.

Space shuttle *Endeavour*

Orbiter Vehicle OV-105. One of three currently operational orbiters in NASA's Space Shuttle Fleet (together with *Atlantis* and *Discovery*), *Endeavour* was constructed by Rockwell International for $2.2 billion as a replacement for *Challenger*, which exploded shortly after take-off in 1986. The most complex machine ever created (with 2 million moving parts and 150 miles of internal wiring), the last shuttle ever built was launched in May 1992 and has completed 22 missions in its seventeen-year service. *Endeavour*, *Atlantis* and *Discovery* are due to fly eight more missions (to date they have over 278 million miles on the clock) before being decommissioned in September 2010 – making way for the US government's new Constellation space programme that intends to return man to the Moon in 2020 and thereafter to Mars. In preparation for their decommissioning, NASA advertised the sale of the three shuttles in December 2008. Price: $36 million each. Bidders were advised that a further $6 million would be required to transport the shuttle to the nearest airport atop a specially-fitted 747.

Haile Selassie's visitors' book

Visitors' book belonging to Haile Selassie (1892–1975), emperor of Ethiopia,
including photographs and signatures of various heads of state – including
the Queen – who visited the country during his imperial rule. Haile Selassie
was Ethiopia's regent from 1916 to 1930, then emperor from 1930 to 1974.
He is also revered as the religious symbol for God incarnate among the
Rastafari movement. The movement, which began in Jamaica in the 1930s,
perceives Haile Selassie as a messianic figure who will lead the people of
Africa and the African Diaspora to a golden age of peace, righteousness
and prosperity. The book was sold at auction in December 2008 by J. P.
Humbert of Towcester, England, for £1,600.

Presidential absence note

On 10 June 2009 a meeting at the Green Bay town hall, Wisconsin, was attended by President Barack Obama. When Mr John Corpus rose to ask a question, he explained to the President that he was attending the meeting with his 10-year-old daughter Kennedy, who was missing school. While giving his response to Mr Corpus, President Obama scribbled a note and handed it to the young absconder. It read: 'To Kennedy's teacher. Please excuse Kennedy's absence ... she's with me. [signed] Barack Obama'. Price: Free.

Apple's first sign

The very first brand sign (100" × 22.5") used by Steve Jobs and Steve
Wozniak to promote their fledgling start-up, Apple Computer Co.,
at the first trade shows they attended in 1976, and which remained
in service for years outside the company's headquarters in Cupertino,
California. Apple was founded on 1 April 1976 by Steve Jobs, Steve
Wozniak and Ronald Wayne to sell the Apple I personal computer kit.
They were hand-built by Steve Wozniak in the living room of Jobs's
parents' home, and the Apple I was first shown to the public at the
Homebrew Computer Club. Eventually, 200 computers were built.
Last year Apple Computers achieved over $24bn in gross sales. Sold at
auction by Alexander Autographs on 11 June 2009 for $20,000.

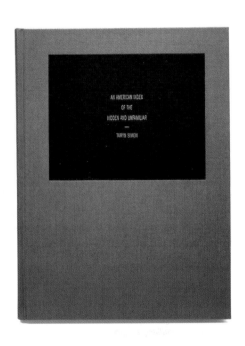

AN AMERICAN INDEX
OF THE
HIDDEN AND UNFAMILIAR
—
TARYN SIMON

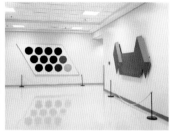

An American Index of the Hidden and Unfamiliar by Taryn Simon

Published by Steidl, 2007. Simon's *American Index* is a photographic documentary of spaces and artefacts that are integral to America's foundation, mythology and daily functioning, but remain inaccessible or unknown to a public audience. Retailed on Amazon.com for £30.49.

Pictures:

(top left): Death-Row Outdoor Recreational Facility, 'The Cage'.
Mansfield Correctional Institution, Ohio

(top right): The Central Intelligence Agency, Displayed Art.
CIA Original Headquarters Builidng, Langley, Virginia

(bottom left): Cryopreservation Unit. The Cryonics Institute.
Clinton Township, Michigan

(bottom right): Research Marjuana Crop Grow Room.
National Products Research, Oxford, Mississippi

Warhead – the Bond film that never was

1976 script for the planned James Bond film _Warhead_, written by
Sean Connery, Bond director Kevin McClory and author Len Deighton.
Due to legal wrangling over the rights to 007, _Warhead_ was never made.
The movie would have starred Sean Connery as James Bond and would
have featured a plan by SPECTRE to detonate a nuclear warhead under
Wall Street, using a robotic shark as the delivery system. Joining Bond
would have been regulars like Ernst Stavros Blofeld, Felix Leiter,
Moneypenny, M and Q. Bond's diversions would have been Justine
Lovesit and Fatima Blush (Fatima would later feature with Connery
in _Never Say Never Again_). In his 2007 book _The Battle For Bond_, Robert
Sellers describes this script as 'one of the great unfilmed scripts in cinema
history'. Sold at auction by Christie's on 4 December 2008 for £46,850.

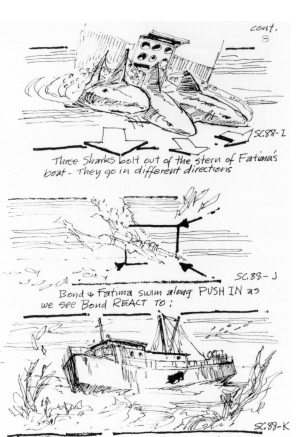

SC.88-I

Three Sharks bolt out of the stern of Fatima's
boat - They go in different directions

SC.88-J

Bond & Fatima swim along PUSH IN as
we see Bond REACT TO;

SC.88-K

Bond's P.O.V. - We see a sunken boat

MI6 camera

In September 2008, a 28-year-old man from Hemel Hempstead bought a Nikon Coolpix camera on eBay for £17. On later downloading his own holiday snaps from the device, he discovered it contained photos, names and fingerprints of terror suspects, images of missiles and rocket launchers and a document, marked 'Top Secret', giving the details of the encrypted computer system used by MI6 agents in the field. He told local police about the find and was shocked when Special Branch officers arrived at his home days later to seize his new purchase. The material found on the camera was reported to be related to 46-year-old Abdul al-Hadi al-Iraqi, a high-ranking al-Qaeda member, who was captured by the CIA in 2007. Neil Doyle, author of *Terror Base UK*, said: 'These are MI6 documents relating to an operation against al-Qaeda insurgents in Iraq. It's jaw-dropping that they got into the public domain. Not only do they divulge secrets about operations, operating systems and previously unheard-of MI6 departments, but they could put lives at risk.'

'Keep Calm and Carry On' poster

In 2005, Stuart Manley, a Northumberland bookseller, discovered an old poster amidst a box of books he'd bought at auction. Emblazoned against a bold red background and featuring the crown of King George VI, the message charmed Mr Manley and his wife, and they decided to have it framed and hung in their shop, Barter Books, in Alnwick. What they did not know was that the poster was a rare example of one of three posters (the other two being 'Freedom Is in Peril' and 'Your Courage, Your Cheerfulness, Your Resolution Will Bring Us Victory'), designed by the government in 1939 to stiffen the sinews of a nation on the brink of war. Millions of the latter two were printed and circulated but 'Keep Calm...' (intended for the truly dark days of impending defeat or invasion) was never displayed. There are thought to be only two copies in existence. In any case, customers to the shop saw the appeal of the poster and started ordering copies in their hundreds. With the onslaught of an historic recession in 2008, the craze went national, and the slogan appeared on everything from mugs to mouse-pads, T-shirts to pencil-cases, and even the front cover of *The Lady* magazine. By early 2009, the 70-year-old abandoned image had become a peculiarly modern icon of a nation's response to adversity. The poster is still retailed by Barter Books for £3.50.

'Now Panic and Freak Out' T-shirt
Conceived by Olly Moss. Sold by
Threadless.com in April 2009 for $15.

A copy of the Government War Book

On 23 June 2009, what was once the most secret of all British government documents was released in full. A Cold War action plan drawn up by the government more than 40 years ago and updated until the early 1990s, the 'Government War Book' sets out in minute detail how the country would have been administered in the event of a Third World War. The mandates contained in the book – including the rounding up of subversives, the takeover of the BBC and the devolution of government to twelve regional police states (each run from underground bunkers by a cabinet minister, a senior military figure, a judge and a police chief) – were ritually practised by civil servants every two years. One exercise, in September 1968, envisaged a Soviet landing on the moon, the forced crashing of an American airliner and a Warsaw Pact invasion of Austria, West Germany, Finland, Turkey, Greece, Italy and the Danish islands. The darkest hypothetical scenario of all, however, was that known as 'R-Hour', the moment of ultimate hopeless extremis, when all the nuclear weapons available to the nation would be unleashed upon the enemy. In this case, the government officials involved were doing nothing less than rehearsing the end of the world. The newly released sections of the 'War Book' are available from the National Archives at Kew. Price: Free.

Miles Davis's trumpet

Martin Committee trumpet with dark green metallic finish (serial number 203005) owned and played by Miles Davis (1926–1991). Given to Ray Robinson (son of Sugar Ray Robinson, a close friend of boxing-fan Davis) in 1966, the trumpet was sold by Julien's Auctions in July 2008 for $25,000.

Michelangelo's first painting

The Torment of Saint Anthony by Michelangelo di Lodovico Buonarroti Simoni (1475–1564). Oil and tempera painting on a wood panel depicting scaly, horned, winged demons trying to wrest the saint from the sky. Bought for $2 million by an art dealer at a Sotheby's auction in the summer of 2008, the painting was then taken to New York's Metropolitan Museum of Art, where experts confirmed that not only was it by Michelangelo, but that it was likely to be the artist's earliest work. Michelangelo painted the picture when he was only twelve or thirteen years old. Acquired by the Kimbell Art Museum in Fort Worth, Texas, in May 2009 for an undisclosed sum, *The Torment of Saint Anthony* will be displayed from autumn 2009.

Hector Husselby's birthday present

Pencil and crayon on paper, 2008. Husselby, aged 6, after consulting his mother on what might make a suitable artistic subject for his godfather's birthday present, was advised to just draw something his Uncle Jolyon liked. The resulting artwork, entitled simply *Fags*, was exhibited and sold at Form 2B's charity art auction at Le Meunier Sacred Heart School, West London, in November 2008 for £18 (to his godfather).

If you'd like to contact us with any ideas for items that might be good to include in a future edition of 'ownable things', then we'd be delighted to hear from you. Please email us at:

Jolyon@jolyonandmarcus.com

Marcus@2oltd.com

With many thanks,

Jolyon and Marcus

INDEXES

Price Index

Free A copy of the Government War Book

Free 'Jackson'

Free Presidential absence note

US$1 ZWD$100 billion banknote

£3.50 'Keep Calm and Carry On' poster

$15 'Now Panic and Freak Out' T-shirt

£8.99 *Fleet Foxes* by Fleet Foxes

£10 MoD 'HM Forces' Action Men

€15 M.Dutriez's jam

£17 MI6 camera

£18 Hector Husselby's birthday present

£20 Mindarus Harringtoni

£30.49 *An American Index* by Taryn Simon

US$33 ZWD$100 trillion banknote

$40 Black Canary Barbie

£44.99 Kennedy car, Dallas, 22 November 1963

$50 Obama posters by Shepard Fairey (other versions $100 and $500)

$50 Apartment in the Panorama of the City of New York

$100 'Force' trainer

€190 Baskerville 10 typeface

$300 *Playboy*, Braille edition

£260 Kate Moss's bed

$365 Holy water sprinkler by Parker

£300 Sir Peter Viggers's duck house

£450 (per tonne) Smog-eating cement

£1,080 The last Woolworth's cheque

£1,150 General Gordon's secret message

$1,000-$1,500 Michael Jackson's Dance Game

$1,875 Jack by Jackie

$1,905 Honda Cub 50th anniversary edition

$2,000 James Brown's lighter

$2,400 X-ray glasses

$2,000–$2,500 'Bat-zooka'

£2,000 Rare bead necklace by Marcel Wanders

$2,000–$3,000 Pamela Anderson's swimsuit

$3,000 Blackstock picture

$3,000 Mr Chu's dog collar

$5,000 King Kong's head

£4,000 Photograph of Jonathan the tortoise

£7,500 The last picture of Marilyn Monroe

$7,500 Air Jordan IV UNDEFEATED trainers

£5,500 Last picture of Florence Nightingale

£5,600 Churchill's in-flight 'whisky' breakfast

£6,325 Del Boy's van

£7,725 Oscar Wilde's cane

€9,500 Pope John Paul II's 'Popemobile'

$15,000 Seven-legged spider by David Thorne

£13,999 Steve McQueen's desert racer

$19,375 Jimi Hendrix's wah-wah pedal

$20,000 Dean Martin's tux

$20,000 Apple's first sign

£15,700 Queen's head stamp cast

$25,000 Dylan's mouth organ

$25,000 Miles Davis's trumpet

£17,000 'Good versus Evil' football table

£17,200 Collection of Britain's last hangman

£20,000 W. G. Grace's bat

$36,099 'Original' Levi's

$40,000 Rommel's 'P45'

$42,700 Steve McQueen's motorcycle licence

$40,000–$60,000 Captain Cook's boomerang

$61,000 Bobby Fischer's library

$68,000 Your complete human genome

€50,000 Enigma cipher machine

€53,500 Smoking Hepburn stamp

£46,850 *Warhead* – the Bond film

£50,000 The real Mr Darcy

$89,500 The 'Wicked' Bible

$70,000–$90,000 Apollo 11 lunar surface map

€80,500 Eiffel Tower staircase

$78,300 £1 million banknote

$138,000 Pat Garrett's gun

£90,000 *Titanic* binoculars storeroom key

£111,500 007 Lotus Esprit

£140,000 Lamborghini police car

$200,000 A ticket to space

$207,743 Luke Skywalker's lightsabre

$238,000 Gatsby's Rolls

$250,000 *Enola Gay* pilot's uniform

$317,200 First Superman comic

£265,000 Uncle Monty's cottage

£275,000 *Ulysses* first edition

£300,000 Hard disk of MPs' expenses

£313,250 *Bill With Shark* by Damien Hirst

$596,000 Einstein's watch

£1m The Corpus Clock

£1.2m Alexander Sims's future earnings (20% share of)

£1.27m Gandhi's glasses

£1.8m Unnamed pure-bred female camel

$3,250,000 Frank Sinatra's house

$5.2m Rodin's *The Thinker*

€5,500,000 Knights Templar chateau

£5 million Secret MI6 tunnels

£5.4m Lucian Freud's *Bacon*

$7.9m *Beverly Hills Housewife* by David Hockney

€9,020,000 1957 Ferrari 250 Testa Rossa

$12.95m The Kauffmann House

$36m Space shuttle *Endeavour*

£40m 'Great Britain'

€600m Château Latour

hundreds of $millions Continental shelf

$1bn $1 billion artwork by Michael Marcovici

street value: Super Lemon Haze

highest bidder: Obama's Illinois senate seat

highest bidder: SS *United States*

undisclosed sum: Michelangelo's first painting

Items are listed in price order using July 2009 exchange rates.

Alphabetical Index

The authors would very much like to thank the following for their help in the creation of this book:

Christie's, Sotheby's, Bonhams, Antiquorum, Alexander Autographs, Profiles in History, Crosby Doe Associates, Julien's Auctions, Mullocks Auctioneers, Drouot, Spink of London, RM Auctions, Rock Island Auctions, Savills, Cuttlestones Fine Art Auctioneers, Elegant Resorts, Henry Aldridge & Sons, Vintagepens.com, Minichamps, Olly Moss, Breker.com, Knome, Andrew Smith Auctioneers, Frank Marshall & Co, Damien Hirst, Otakar Karlas, Lyon & Turnbull, Moore Allen & Innocent, Dreweatts, Bella Union, Honda, Comic Connect, Richard Wright of Chicago, Sylvie Robaglia, Andrea Jemolo, Roman Salicki, Shepard Fairey, Mattel, La Perla International Living, Lucian Freud, Metisse Motorcycles, Schlegel, Character Options, Greatsite.com, Artcurial, Guy Walters, Angie Voluti, Virgin Gallactic, Michael Marcovici, Garde Rail Gallery, Britishsportsmuseum.com, Queen's Museum of Art, John C. Taylor, Advanced Intelligence, NASA, Taryn Simon, J. P. Humbert, M. Dutriez's Jam, The Kimbell Art Museum, Judy & Brian Harden, SamAshMusic. com, Uncle Milton Industries, Jill Husselby, Harry Stourton, Charlotte Goldsmith, Gessica Finaurini, Carla Matoses, Gavin Kennedy, Andrew Franklin and Paul Forty. And with special thanks to Mina Fry.